Barbara Stieff

Hundertwasser
for Kids

Harvesting Dreams in the Realm of the Painter-King

Prestel Verlag

Munich · London · New York

532 THE LION OF VENICE, 1962

Hundertwasser always numbered his pictures; for him, the work number formed part of the picture's name. Under the illustrations in this book you will find the (picture number), followed by the title of the picture and the year in which it was painted.

Contents

Just follow these suggestions!

Do you know Hundertwasser?

Friedensreich Hundertwasser was an **artist**. He had a lively imagination and plenty of ideas. Some of them became **pictures** and some became **buildings**. And he turned many others into **messages** to the people around him, which he either wrote down or talked about. This book is about his pictures and the houses which he designed, about the ideas he developed and the questions he asked. And it is about **you**.

"… pictures, houses, ideas and questions, that's all very well," you are probably thinking, "but **ME**? This book is about **ME**? That's not possible. He didn't even know me and I didn't know Mr Hundertwasser either. How could he possibly have been thinking about me?"
That's quite right, of course. But all the same, this book has a lot to do with you …

 You can be the son or daughter of a  king and dance around in spirals at a party and have lots of fun! Where is the "shoe-box house" and who lives in it?
Is there any treasure buried there?
And who is it who sends you postcards while at sea using a "ship of wishes"?

Do you want to find out more about these secrets? All it takes is the time you need to read this book. You can open it and close it again whenever you feel like it. So how long it takes you is something which you can decide for yourself.

How it all began...

Friedrich "Fritz" Stowasser with his mother ...

Friedensreich Hundertwasser – like everyone else – was once a child, too. And at the very beginning, of course, was the day he was born – that's pretty obvious! Whether it was on a sunny or a rainy day, nobody knows. All we do know is that he was born on **15 December, 1928** in **Vienna,** the capital of Austria. At that time, the people in Austria were going through difficult times and many of them were very poor.

... in a paddle boat ...

His family was not rich, either. His father died young and so he lived with his mother and aunts in a little flat. His name was really ***Friedrich Stowasser,*** but his family called him ***Fritz***. He thought up that name Friedensreich Hundertwasser for himself much later on.

... and in the garden.

When he was eleven years old, war broke out: the **Second World War.** It was a terrible time. There was not much food and everywhere there was fighting and shooting; bombs fell on cities, whole areas of the city were destroyed and everybody was very afraid.

When Hundertwasser went for a walk through Vienna at the end of the war he passed houses which had been completely bombed or partly destroyed. The streets had been ripped up, too; they were full of potholes and bomb craters in which the rainwater gathered. And in these puddles, new life started to emerge. If you looked carefully you could see the larvae of insects and tadpoles. Soon grass began to grow out of the cracks in the asphalt, and between the heaps of rubble of the ruined houses you could see plants taking root. They were the delicate shoots of bushes and trees.

This is what Hundertwasser looked like when he was about six years old.

All that impressed Hundertwasser greatly at the time. Like everyone else he had longed so much for peace, and these little insects and young plants were a sign for him: the war was over – now there would be no more destruction and things could be rebuilt.

A love of nature was important to him throughout his life.

He wanted to protect nature and treat it with respect; and he wanted to understand how things grew and why things died. This was the theme of his paintings and drawings; this was to become the subject of speeches he gave and made him want to build and live in houses which were in harmony with nature.

The desire to discover and preserve the wonders of nature and life was very strong even when he was a child. During his hikes in the Vienna Woods he picked flowers which he pressed between the pages of heavy books. But they lost their magnificent colours. And so he said to himself:

"If I paint flowers instead of pressing them, they will keep their colour."

JW 33 (XX) SMALL BUNCH OF SPRING FLOWERS, 1944

It was during the war, as a schoolboy, that Fritz painted this idyllic picture of the Danube Canal near Vienna. It does not show the destruction of the war, however, but rather the beauty of a summer's day in Vienna.

JW 69 (11) DANUBE CANAL WITH FERRY SEEN TOWARDS FRIEDENSBRÜCKE, 1945

A further encouragement to paint came from his **stamp collection**. These tiny little pictures were Fritz's most precious treasures. He looked at them again and again. They came from faraway countries and were so beautiful to look at. And Fritz Stowasser wanted to learn to paint just as beautifully as the artists who had designed the stamps.

Do you have some treasure? Something which makes you secretly very happy and which you take great care of and keep hidden away?

Look at page 89!

Occupation: Artist

Fritz Stowasser loved **painting** – so much so that he wanted to make it his **career**. At the beginning his mother didn't think very much of the idea at all; she would have preferred him to study something else: to have "a proper job". Parents are often like that. But Fritz had his own ideas and he insisted on following them through. When he was twenty years old, he decided to take the entrance examination for the **Academy of Fine Arts**.* He passed the exam and started to study painting.

Fritz Stowasser aged 20

* An academy is a sort of school or university.

That was a completely new phase in his life! And because he had now become an artist he wanted a new name as well. An **artist's name**. He thought of the time when the war was finally over and there was peace once more throughout the land, and new life began to emerge in the puddles of water in the countless craters. "Frieden" is the German word for peace and "Reich" a realm or kingdom; the word "Sto" (from Stowasser) means "hundred" in the Slavic language, and "Wasser" is the German for water. And so Friedrich Stowasser became **Friedensreich Hundertwasser.**

JW 135 28 SELF-PORTRAIT, 1948

If you could choose a new name for yourself, what would it be? Perhaps it wouldn't be an artist's name, but the name of a Red Indian or simply a nickname.

What are the things you like best? If you were to use their names, everyone would immediately know what you like. Perhaps someone would then be called "Pauline Pizza" or "Simon Smiley Face" or "Lizzy Cloudchild" – or someone else, who loved his pet rabbit, might choose the name "Snufflenose Furry McGraw" or "Thumper Softpaw Jones".

That would be quite something, don't you think?

So what would your name be? Why not make one up!

_____

_____

_____

_____

By the way, Hundertwasser didn't stay very long at the Academy. He had a mind of his own! After only a few months he set off on a journey. He decided he would rather see the world and discover what life was about and learn the skills he needed to paint by actually painting. And so he carried on learning throughout his entire life because he never stopped painting.

A mind of his own

You have probably already heard the expression: "He has a mind of his own."

What does it mean?

Whose mind would we have if not our own?

Just imagine!

You can try out what it would be like to be someone else, with someone else's mind. Have you got a photo of yourself? Now find a few newspapers or magazines and cut out the heads from some of the photos. Then lay them on top of your head on the photo, and see what it looks like.

How do you feel when someone else's head is sitting on your body? Or maybe even several strange heads. It must look very funny, but is it still you? If you were to show the picture to a friend, would he or she immediately recognise that is it you? Is there another head which would suit you better than the one you have?

Friedensreich Hundertwasser had a mind of his own. He wanted to become an artist and so he actually became one, even though his mother thought it wasn't really a proper job. But he clung to his dream. For him, it was very important to believe in what he could do and to make his own ideas come true. He wanted to explain that to other people too, to invite them to try it out for themselves, but often they didn't want to listen to him. That is how it is with some people

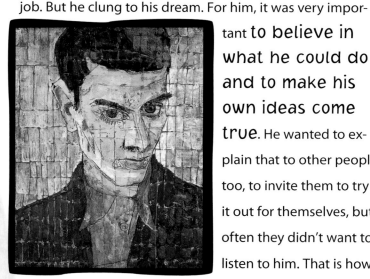

91 *Checkered Self-Portrait, 1950*

when you tell them something new or unexpected, even if it is something nice.

Friedensreich was a free spirit, a "lateral thinker", someone who challenged people. He wanted people to feel for themselves, to discover what they really wanted, and then to express it. Maybe you are thinking now: "But what is so bad about that?" That's a good question!

left: Hundertwasser's studio in Spiegelgasse in Vienna, August 1973

Let's look at an example. If you go out for a meal, let's say to a pizzeria, you will find there are various items listed on the menu:

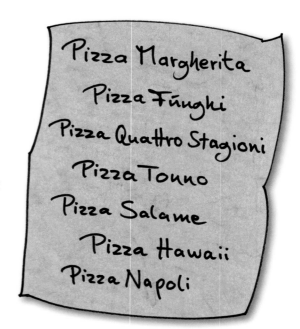

Pizza Margherita
Pizza Funghi
Pizza Quattro Stagioni
Pizza Tonno
Pizza Salame
Pizza Hawaii
Pizza Napoli

You can choose from these different sorts of pizza which somebody or other thought up some time ago. **There's not much to think about there, is there? It's all very easy.**

But now imagine you arrive at the pizzeria and the pizza which you would really like to eat isn't on the menu.

You order: **"Waiter, I should like a square pizza made of cake dough with strawberry mousse and pear drops."**
The waiter may think you have made a joke and then he will say that he is sorry, but they don't have a pizza like that. "Not yet!" you think to yourself, because if you were to set to work in the kitchen and bake a pizza like that, then of course it would exist. (Perhaps you will have to eat it on your own, because no one wants to try it. That won't matter – there will be all the more for you!)

That is what many people find so difficult, when someone turns up with his or her own ideas. Things are simply not the way they expect them to be. **You have to think about things and possibly even change something.** Some people don't like that. If I want to eat something which isn't on the menu, I have to make it myself. And if I am too lazy or it simply doesn't seem that important, then I shall have to put up with Pizza Margherita, Napoli or Hawaii. **If everyone were to react like that, nothing new would ever be invented,** and that would be a shame! There wouldn't be any bicycles, in-line skates or air mattresses, no computer games – not even a Pizza Hawaii …

Hundertwasser in his studio, 1973

You know that Friedensreich Hundertwasser
was not a pizza chef, but an **artist**.
He thought about all sorts of things:

about painting ...

*HUNDERTWASSER TOWER –
ARCHITECTURE MODEL,
2000*

how people might live,

The artists with his home-made shoes; he took the photo himself in 1952

what sort of clothes they might wear,

Hundertwasser with clothes he had designed, 1960

Time and again he would ask for things which were not on the menu, things which hadn't been invented yet. People found him very strange and often rather difficult. But he never expected everyone to share his enthusiasm for his new ideas. He liked them himself, of course.

The artist having a bath in the New Zealand jungle

●●● how we can live in harmony with nature and lots of other things.

Hundertwasser's home-made summer and winter shoes

It's very important that we all have a mind of our own. The only thing is, you can never actually see what's going on in the other person's head.

In order to make our unusual, maybe even fabulous ideas visible, we have to be allowed to talk about them or possibly even carry them out.

If we do that the world will become a richer, more interesting and more beautiful place!

Simply unique

Look around you! Then you will discover **things which people have made**, but also **things which come from nature**. And now look and see if you can find ———— any perfectly straight lines ————. So straight , ———— that they must have been drawn with a ruler ————. Do you find them in things which people have made, or in nature?

What is nature, anyway? **Nature** is everything which exists or which is formed without help from people: the mountains, valleys, rivers, the sea, the sun and the moon, plants and animals. All those things are there without we humans having to do anything at all.

And then there are things which **people have made** and thought up: cars, streets, houses, clothes, washing machines, school bags, stereo systems, bunk beds, crayons, hair slides, wooden spoons, computers …

Friedensreich in front of a high-rise concrete block – a monster construction with absolutely straight lines

But what about people themselves?

Were we invented or are we a part of nature? We are born, we grow and we get older. Although we are a part of nature, we spend most of our time not outside, but in buildings made by people.

That is something which made Friedensreich Hundertwasser think a great deal. He sensed that we are getting further and further away from nature, as if we didn't belong to it. He noticed that people were not happy when they have lost their connection with nature. That is what he thought. Let's look a little closer at this idea!

**How can that be?
Why are people
unhappy and ill?**

*Hundertwasser with a bent ruler, 1985. (The ruler was bent
like that during a fire in a flat.)*

Hundertwasser explains the difference between nature and things
which humans have made like this:

"In nature there are no straight lines drawn with a ruler."

He didn't like straight lines. He believed that whenever we see a ▬▬▬▬
we feel uncomfortable because it is not natural. Straight lines make us
unhappy and make us believe we are part of a man-made world. They
make us **forget that we are a part of nature.**
In nature everything, every flower, every snowflake, every blade of grass,
is unique. There is never a second one which is exactly the same as the
first. Every object is special. With people it is the same. Each person is
unique and there will never be another one who is exactly like him or her.
Not even twins are truly identical, they just look very, very like each other.

One day Friedensreich Hundertwasser went for a bicycle ride. And he noticed that he did not ride in a straight line although the street was completely straight. He kept swerving slightly to the right or the left. He rode along a curvy path, sometimes faster and sometimes slower. And he thought that even this simple track which he was riding along was unique. Not unique in the sense of outstanding or wonderful, but simply just **unique, unlike any other.** All people cycle along curved lines, but no two curves are ever exactly alike.

132/IX   CYCLIST IN THE RAIN, 1951

We cannot even retrace our own tracks.

You can try it if you like. Write your **name** on a sheet of paper. Then take a second sheet and try to write your name in **exactly the same way again**. You won't be able to do it — you can prove it by laying the sheets one on top of the other and holding them up to the light. Isn't that amazing! Each time you write your name, it becomes a new, unique signature.

Hundertwasser painting

The phenomenal spiral

Friedensreich Hundertwasser didn't like straight lines, but he was fascinated by **spirals**. Spirals occur all the time in his pictures. He painted them all his life. He saw them as a **symbol of life and nature**.

We often use **symbols** in everyday life. Symbols are **signs** which stand for something else. For example, when you see a ♡ you think of **love**, and when you see a skull it is a warning:

Take care! Danger!

If you look around you, you will notice there are lots of different symbols. They are pictures which tell us something.

(315) SNAIL SLEEP OF AN AUSTRIAN LANDSCAPE, 1957

Why not invent a symbol of your own? What does it look like?
Which colours do you like best and which shapes? Will your symbol be blue and round or will it have green and yellow stripes with tassels?
Draw your very own symbol!

23

Why is the spiral a symbol for life?

At first sight, spirals are not very easy to find – and yet they are all around us.

Have a look! If you look around you, don't forget that life is part of **nature**. In man-made things the spiral is much less common.
Can you imagine that you even have some spirals in you?
A hint: They are not very easy to spot because they are so small.

Have you found any? There is one on each fingertip! And even our ears look quite like spirals too, don't they? If you compare your fingerprints with other people's you will discover something very exciting: every person in the whole world has fingerprints which are unlike anyone else's. No two sets of fingerprints are alike. In spite of the fact that there are almost 6.4 billion people living on Earth! For thousands of years a thumbprint has therefore been used as a signature.

Granny 67 years old

Dad 46 years old

Mum 44 years old

David 16 years old

Alicia 9 years old

In order to see the spirals on your fingers more clearly, you can cover them with a small amount of paint or press them on an ink pad and then make fingerprints on a sheet of paper.

An unborn baby lies in its mother's womb like a tiny spiral. After it is born, as it grows and gets bigger, it unfolds like a flower. Tiny babies are often still curled up like a spiral as they lie in their cots.

And even though we have learned to sit up straight and walk upright, we still often lie curled up in bed when we go to sleep. We feel safe when we lie like that.

(170) THE GARDEN OF THE HAPPY DEAD, 1953

Unborn baby in the womb

A fern unrolls

If we look at nature all around us we can find lots of examples of spirals: plants, animals, elements …

Snail

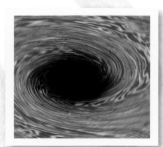

Whirlpool

Spiral nebula in space

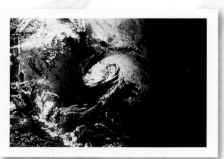

Whirlwind, photographed from space

So there are spirals all over the place, great big ones and little tiny ones.

They begin at the beginning, in the middle, at the central point, and they turn further and further towards the outside. The spiral itself could carry on like that for ever, but when we draw one, we have to stop when we get to the edge of the paper. There we can't see them any more, but we know that they carry on and on. Life is like that too.

It starts as a tiny point when we are conceived.

We grow and are born. We develop and become a child, a teenager, an adult.

Then maybe we have children ourselves.

Then we get older and die.

But dying is only like the edge of the sheet of paper on which we are drawing. We cannot see our body any more, but the spiral of our soul keeps on turning on and on, for ever and ever.

That was how Friedensreich Hundertwasser saw it. That is why he loved the spiral so much and was so enthusiastic about it. And that is why he drew spirals in his pictures, again and again.

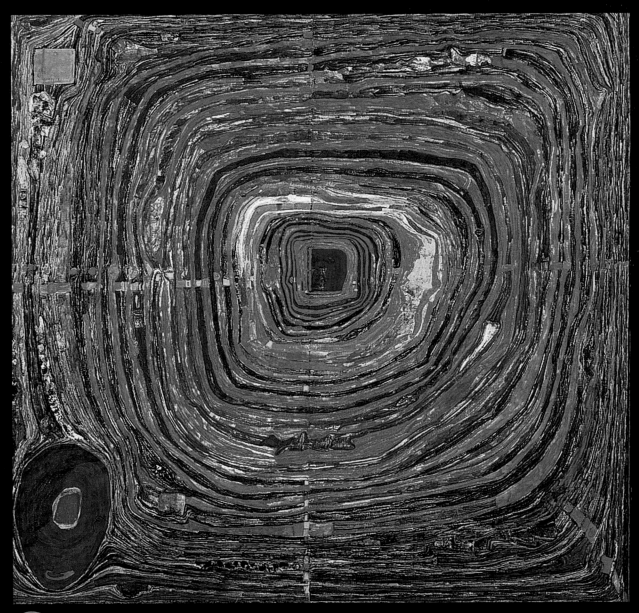

224 THE BIG WAY, 1955

Painting is dreaming

We need several different things to paint:
We need **paints**, something to paint on and an idea.

I'm sure you have often done some painting. Our first pictures are usually made with finger paints or brightly coloured wax crayons, because small children still find it very difficult to hold a pencil. But they paint all the same because it is an activity they enjoy and because it feels so wonderful to makes things with paint and to play around. Later on, we learn how to use different tools like pencils and paintbrushes.

What **materials** can we use to paint? Which ones do you know? Have a quick think – have you already tried them all out?

Pictures by modern artists often seem to ask us a **riddle**. They are not like photographs which show a bit of our world. **Painters take us with them into their own world**, the world of painting. In Hundertwasser's world there are unusual things to see. And lots of things to discover.

Look at page 90!

A head with many eyes ...

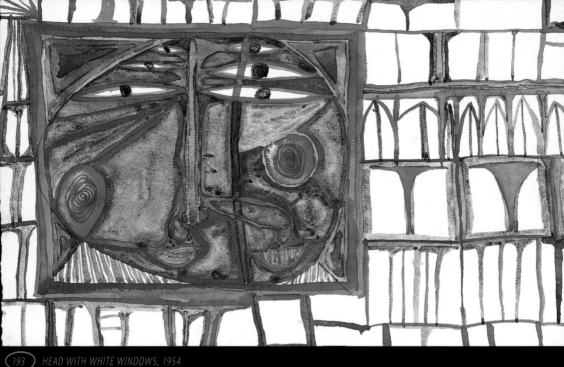

193   HEAD WITH WHITE WINDOWS, 1954

... a "double cat" ...

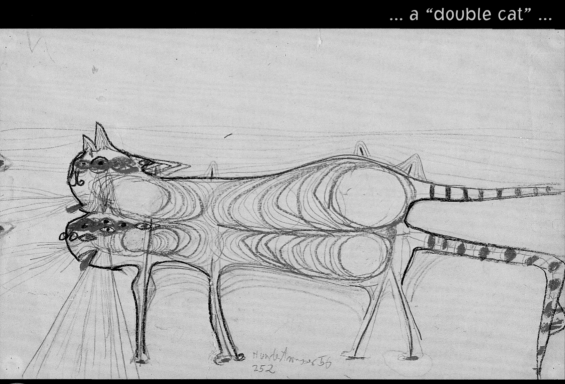

252   DOUBLE CAT, 1956

HUNDERTWASSER 1956

LANDSCAPE WITH VIOLET SUN, 1956

... round houses with spiral façades ...

566 *THE THREE HOUSES OF ATLANTIS, 1963*

... a head and a ship with trees growing out of them ...

687 *COLUMBUS LANDS IN INDIA, 1969*

TENDER DINGHI, 1982

... two cyclists in a snake's stomach ...

956 DADAKULACI – LATICAUDA COLUBRINA (Giant Banded Sea Krait) 1994

"To paint is to dream. When I paint, I dream.
When the dream is over,
I cannot remember what it was about.
But the picture remains.
That is the harvest of my dreams."

Hundertwasser painted very slowly. He often spent years on a picture until he felt that it was really finished. Of course, he didn't spend the whole time sitting and working away on just one painting. He worked on it a bit, put it to one side and began another picture; then he went on a journey and when he got back he would get the picture out and carry on working at it again. **His pictures grew gradually, like plants.** At the beginning there was not much to see, just a few lines or surfaces. And gradually he would add more and more details; the colours would become brighter and the picture developed.

Hundertwasser's paintings grew gradually and slowly. He called his way of painting "vegetative painting".

Vegetative means, on the one hand, that it has something to do with plants – and, on the other, that it is something **which does not happen according to our will**. A bit like dreaming, in fact. Pictures are formed in our heads, but they are not pictures which we have thought up. They just appear. That is a very strange process, but it can be very exciting and bring a lot of pleasure.

If you want to, you can try this out as a game. You need a blindfold for your eyes and a partner whom you trust. When your eyes have been bound, you will be turned around until you have lost your bearings. Now you can try to explore the room you are in. Where is the door, the window, the sofa? First of all you are very nervous and just stand still. You listen very hard and stretch out your arms to feel your way around. Perhaps you will suddenly become aware of the smells in the room. Then you start to move very slowly, very carefully. Slowly you feel your way and your partner watches out that you do not hurt yourself – that will give you courage and a sense of security. You cannot do anything wrong because he or she will lead you safely. When you have had enough, swap places. Then you can find out what it is like to lead someone carefully and to look after him or her.

Friedensreich Hundertwasser felt like that when he painted. He said:

"If the artist is not completely surprised at what he is painting, then it isn't a good picture. I want to be surprised by my own pictures. I want to keep on discovering my own pictures."

"Painting is something tremendous. It gives us the possibility of penetrating unexplored regions which are far, far away from us."

In just the same way that you explored the room with the blindfold on your eyes Hundertwasser **explored his pictures.** He had an idea, a dream or a feeling which he wanted to paint. But he didn't just grab his paintbrush. First of all, he sat down in front of the canvas. And then he started, very slowly and carefully. First of all he had to find the **right way** and the **right colours** for his picture. And at some point he suddenly had the feeling that he was **being led.** Then he didn't need to think any more, everything happened automatically. He once described it like this:

> "When I paint, I do not try to force the process. I allow myself to be led. That way I cannot make any mistakes."

Many artists, or even people who can allow themselves to be completely absorbed by something or other, say that they have the same feeling. Have you ever had such an experience? That you were concentrating on something so completely that you didn't notice time passing, or you didn't hear when someone called you?

Hundertwasser painting, 1989

When that happens we don't think any more, we simply carry on doing whatever it is. Afterwards we may even be surprised at what we have achieved without it being exhausting or boring. It is as if someone had taken your hand and led you. Nobody can really explain who it is and where it comes from.

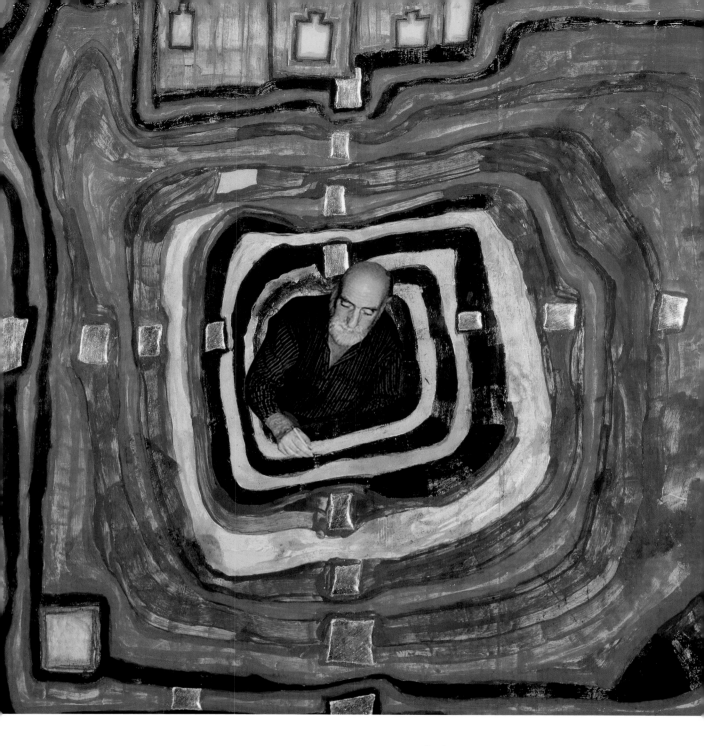

Friedensreich Hundertwasser said that painting was a **religious activity**, and he was quite sure that it was a **divine power** which was leading him.

When you look at this picture, one of the first things you notice is bound to be the bright colours. All Hundertwasser's paintings are full of colour and life and light.

Hundertwasser especially liked dark-bright colours.

That was an expression he invented because it best describes how he saw them:

"Dunkelbunt means: glowing in pure strong and deep colours a little sad like seen on a rainy day.

On a rainy day the colours begin to glow. That is why a dull day — a rainy day — is for me a fine day. It's a day when I can work. When it is raining I am happy. And when it is raining I know my day can begin!"

Look at page 91!

840   *CIEL COUVERT – LES CIELS D'ICI ET DE LA (Cloudy Sky - The Heavens of Here and There), 1982*

By the way, he liked the words dunkelbunt and Regentag so much that he added them to his name. So then he was called:

Friedensreich Regentag Dunkelbunt Hundertwasser –
Realm of Peace, Rainy Day, Dark-Bright, Hundred Water!

Have you ever noticed how the **colours in nature change**? In the morning, when the sun is just above the horizon, or at midday, when it is high in the sky above our heads and shines most brightly? A forest can change the way it looks at any time, depending on what the light conditions are like. On a cloudy afternoon it looks quite different than on a sunny spring morning. And on a rainy day the colours change yet again.

You can explore this idea if you like. Remember a sunny day, and the colours, and how you felt on that day. Choose the colours in your paint box which best match that feeling and paint a picture. Then put it away so that you can't see it any more. Now think about a rainy day when you were outside. What sort of mood was there then? What were the colours like? If you can't find them in your paint box you will have to mix them. Which colours do you have to mix together to paint the mood on a **rainy day**? It's a fascinating experiment. When you have painted your picture, you can compare your two paintings, the sunny-day picture and the rainy-day picture. Can you see any difference?

 Friedensreich Hundertwasser was an artist of colour.
When he was asked:
"What is it that makes a good picture?"
he answered:

"A good picture is when the picture is full of magic, when you can feel the happiness in it, when it makes you laugh or cry, or when it makes something happen. It should be like a flower or a tree. It should be like Nature. It should be that we miss it when it isn't there."

1961 HUNDERTWASSER
TOKYO

Three skins
The first skin. The body

Our skin surrounds our body and keeps everything together. It is the part of our self which is nearest the outside, the part we can see. All living creatures have a skin which is adapted to suit where they live:

Fish live in water. They usually have a slimy skin of **scales** so that they can glide smoothly through the water.

Birds have **feathers** growing on their skin, which they need in order to be able to fly.

Other animals have thick **fur** to keep them warm.

People have a skin, too, but it is not the same all over. On our faces and in places where we are ticklish, the skin is very sensitive. On our feet, however, we have thicker skin which makes it easier for us to walk. Because it is so thick we don't notice the stones on the ground so much and it doesn't hurt as much when we go barefoot. Imagine if the skin on our feet were as thin as the skin on our faces – we would have to stay in bed all day, or in the bath. But you know what happens to our skin when we lie in the water too long. It begins to wrinkle. After all, we're not fish.

42

The different parts of trees have different sorts of skin, because each part of the tree has a different job:

The trunk determines how big the tree will grow. It has to be strong enough to carry the top of the tree. Mostly the skin is rough: it is a hard, protective **bark**.

Look at page 90!

The bark on the branches is not so thick, because branches must be flexible – otherwise they would break whenever it is stormy and windy.

The **leaves** grow again every year and help the tree to breathe.
The skin on the leaves is the thinnest of all. It even changes its colour according to the season.

The second skin. Our clothes

Since people don't have fur to keep them warm, they invented clothing. **Clothing is our second skin.** We can't choose what sort of first skin we have, we have to put up with the one we were given when we were born. But we can choose our second skin. It is to **protect** us but it also gives us the freedom to **show what sort of people we are.** Boys and girls, men and women wear different clothes. Your clothing also shows whether you are going to school or to the sports field, whether you are going swimming or to bed at night.

You can make a game like this. Write some sentences, like:

A child sleeps in pyjamas.
A bride gets married in a wedding dress.
A diver goes diving in a wetsuit.
A model poses in a bikini.

If you then cut the sentences up with a pair of scissors and put them together in a different order, you will have invented a new fashion:

A diver   sleeps in   a wedding dress

A model   gets married   in pyjamas

Friedensreich Hundertwasser was surprised – even angry, sometimes – that people all dress the same and wear such boring clothes. He especially liked things which were **unique**, unlike anything else. He would have liked to be able to tell just from the clothing what sort of person he was meeting. But people don't want to be noticed, instead of showing their beauty and their uniqueness.

We are all unique and wonderful, and yet we wear such boring, uniform clothes!
He wanted to feel happy when he saw people. He wanted to discover bright colours and patterns, funny hats, unusual shapes, different socks. Since Hundertwasser couldn't buy the sort of clothing he liked anywhere, he sewed it himself or had it made specially.

Hundertwasser always wore odd socks.

Hundertwasser wearing the suit which he designed for the magazine Vogue.

He especially liked vertical stripes.

He described what he found important:

Clothing is like a house, there is no reason for the interior to be less beautiful, less pleasant than the exterior. It is like with pyjamas. Pyjamas are very pleasant. You can sleep in them. You can in my suit, too. You don't feel dressed, you feel enveloped. One feels so much more comfortable in a suit which is too big. The sleeves are too long and not taken in. They cover the hands, but one feels secure. The buttons are all different, too, in their forms as well as colours. My socks are also different. The right and left ones are never alike. The trick is to make them harmonise. I love stripes, and as cloth always throws folds – waves – the visual impression is never that of a stiff straight line, especially if the garment has not been ironed. It is morbid to always want to iron everything. Wash them, yes; iron them, no.

Look at page 92!

Friedensreich Hundertwasser also complained about the fact that nowadays people don't wear hats any more. Hats are so lovely, they are such a great idea. They make people look **taller** and **more important**. Like a king's crown, really.

Everyone should feel like a king, so handsome and important and so full of responsibility for the world in which he or she lives. He said:

"I am a King, I have crowned myself.
I would rather live in a valley with rich kings than in a valley of tears.
One has no need to go far to reach the next paradise, the next kingdom, because paradise starts round the corner at the neighbour's place."

For Friedensreich Hundertwasser life could be a **party**, our surroundings could be **paradise** and all people could be **kings**.

What would that look like? Why not draw a picture of it. What would you look like as a prince or princess?

The next time you have a **party** on your birthday or to celebrate the start of spring, or just because life is so much fun, then you could write your invitations like this:

I should like to invite you to my Royal Ball. Please come as a prince or princess in your finest gown. We are going to dine like kings and amuse ourselves royally.
P.S. Don't forget your crown!

Then you will see how much fun kings and queens have.

Enjoy the party!

844 HATS THAT WEAR YOU, 1982

The third skin. Where we live

The third skin which Friedensreich Hundertwasser talked about was to do with our **flats** and **houses**. Just as our clothes cover our bodies, so our houses are the **outer covering of our private living space**. And in the same way, we should be able to see from the façade of a house, who it is that lives behind the windows.

Here all the windows and balconies are the same, but are the people who live in this block of flats all the same too?

Friedensreich Hundertwasser once said:

"And when I look outside, I see that everything is full of ruled and T-squared misery and everybody is imprisoned, and that is so terrible that it spoils everything for me. I would much prefer looking out somwhere and seeing that it is beautiful everywhere, and it would be important for people to start building their castles themselves."

If you like, you can draw a plan of your **dream home**. How would you like to live? Is your dream home a cottage, a cave or a palace? Is it in a tree, or is it underground or on a cloud? How many rooms do you need for yourself and your family? Would you like some royal pets?
Do they need stables to live in? Dream about the best place in the world and draw a picture of it.

right: The Hundertwasser House in Vienna, 1983-1985
original coauthor Josef Krawina, architect

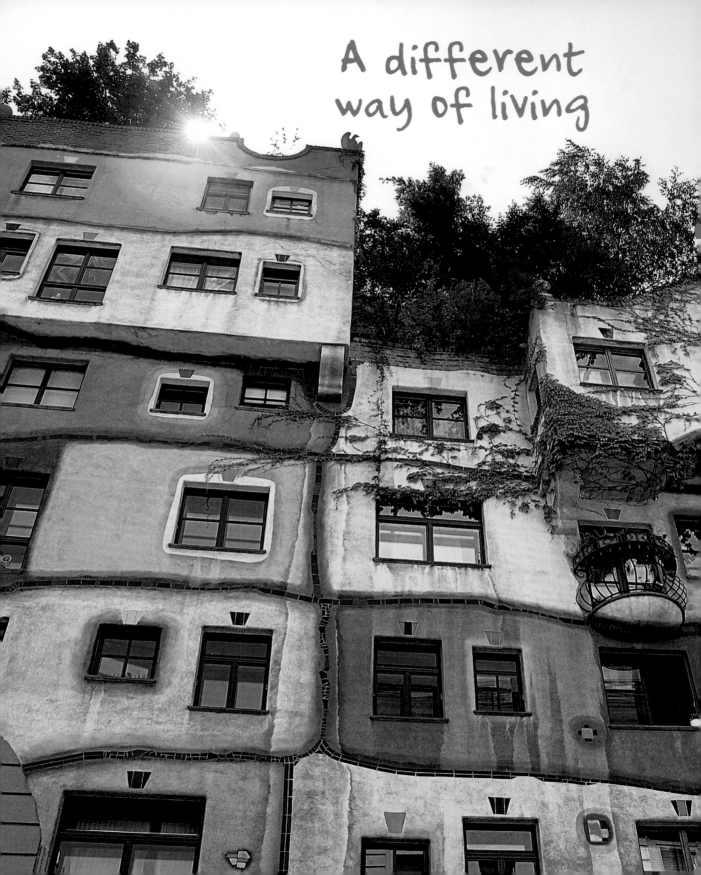

A different
way of living

Friedensreich Hundertwasser didn't just paint; he used his talents in a variety of different areas.

When building **houses and blocks of flats**, it was important for him that his **ideas and dreams** should be reflected in the design. Wherever possible, nature should be incorporated into everyday life.

People should be able to enjoy living in green surroundings and not just breathe in clean air on Sundays on an outing, but all the time, where they lived. Even in a big city. And because, for Hundertwasser, colours were always so important, he thought that a happy place to live also had to glow with bright colours.

left: The Forest Spiral of Darmstadt, 1998–2000

right: In The Meadows Bad Soden, 1990–1993

Window right

Not every family can afford to build its own house. Many people live in a city, in blocks of flats or in a smaller building. Unfortunately, in such cases, you can't determine what the building looks like. An **architect** designs the building the way he thinks it should look. How much space is there? How many people are going to live or work there? How big should the windows be, and how thick the walls? Should the rooms be small and cramped or large and spacious? How do you get from the first floor to the second floor?

This page: Windows in the district heating plant Spittelau, Vienna, 1988–1992

Architects think about lots of questions like these ones and try to find the best answer. Then they draw a **plan**. Then the building is actually built by a **building firm** and **construction workers**.

The **tenants** move into a house which has been **designed and built** by strangers. How can they still show that in every flat, behind every window, there are **unique people** living there?

Balcony and window: The Forest Spiral of Darmstadt, 1999–2000

Hundertwasser thought that was very important. He demanded that everyone should have the right to design the area around his window himself.

He called the idea window right.

The idea was as follows: As far as your arms reach, that is the area round your window which belongs to you as your own private living space. And you can design that space exactly as you like. The tenants can paint it or decorate it with tiles, hang up little flower boxes and grow plants or herbs. You could put a chain around the window like a necklace, or fix metal plates which twinkle in the sun.

If you walked along the street with a friend, you would then be able to say, "Look, up there, behind the purple window with the herbs, that's where I live." Or you could let your friend guess: "Which of the windows is mine, do you think?"

What would your window look like?

You have probably got lots of good ideas. How many different shapes for a window can you think of? How many different patterns and decorations? Unfortunately we can only imagine it nowadays, because, although Hundertwasser demanded the rights for everyone, we're not allowed to do what we like. If you were to design a real house the way you would like it you might get into a lot of trouble. But to see what it might look like you can also make a house out of a shoebox.

Look at page 94!

53

Tree duty

When houses are built, they protect us and provide us with a place to live. Houses are important. But on the place where the house is built, there may have been a field beforehand, or a tree. Before the house was built it was the living space of plants.

Only plants?

What can we do to preserve the living spaces for both forms of life, for humans and plants, so that they can live together side by side? A good question! Friedensreich Hundertwasser had a very simple answer to this question:

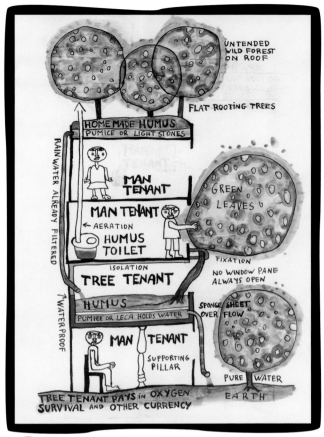

(766) TREE-TENANT, 1976

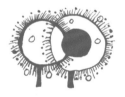

"If I use the living space of the meadow on the ground, I can plant it again on the roof. Then it will have enough space and we have a super roof garden."

All living things have the right to living space, – including trees! And because they cannot speak, they need people to speak for them. People also benefit from living together with plants. Trees produce clean air with their leaves, and they provide shade. Trees swallow up dust and noise and their protective crown of leaves keeps us safe, too. Trees encourage butterflies and birds to live in them, which brings more beauty and joy into our lives. Hundertwasser believed that we have a duty to plant trees. He called it our tree duty.

left: The green citadel of Magdeburg, 2003–2005

Houses can be built in lots of different ways. They can be tall, long, wide, round, square, a single plain colour or all the colours of the rainbow! They can be built of stone, bricks, metal, glass, clay, wood or straw. On his long journeys Hundertwasser came across all sorts of different houses which inspired him to design his own. The most important thing for him was always the connection between man and nature.

*The Eye-Slit House, 1974
(model)*

The Spiral House, 1975
(model)

The Hundertwasser House in Löwengasse in Vienna

The first house which Hundertwasser designed and which was actually built is in Vienna. It was rather hard to persuade the city authorities. He had to draw lots of plans and build lots of models until they finally agreed on what the house should look like.

It was to be a building with 50 flats, with "tree tenants" and roof gardens, with different window designs, brightly coloured and imaginative. It would have onion-shaped towers, crooked lines, mosaics made of broken tiles, oriel windows and balconies. Inside there were to be bright columns which looked solid and reminded the tenants of tree trunks. The house was not to be simply a rectangular block but would consist of sections of different heights so that the silhouette was more varied. It should be a fairy-tale house, as beautiful as the house that Hundertwasser had always dreamed of building.

Look at page 93!

The Hundertwasser House in Vienna, completed in 1985, original coauthor Josef Krawina, architect

A "tree tenant"

In 1983 the foundation stone of the Hundertwasser House was laid.* And then they started to build. It was a big project involving lots of people with different jobs. Many of them helped to build the house. And it was a great success, don't you think?

*A foundation stone is the first stone of a house.

Look at page 92!

The fountain in front of the entrance

A pillar in the entrance hall

Nature + Beauty = Happiness

That looks like a sum doesn't it? Like

$$2 + 2 = 4$$

Nature + Beauty = Happiness.

For Friedensreich Hundertwasser, this formula was the easiest way to express how to find happiness. How to be happy, in fact. **After all, being happy and being lucky are two different things.**

If you have an accident but nothing very dreadful happens, people say: "You were lucky" – but you're not exactly happy all the same. ***Good fortune and happiness mean different things to different people.*** If you are given a cool new skateboard as a present, you'ld be happy. But if your grandfather were given a skateboard for his birthday, he probably wouldn't be as happy about it as you.

For Hundertwasser it was nature and beauty which made him happy.

He said: "Everything is here to be happy on earth.
We have snow and every day a new morning.
We have trees and rain, hope and tears.
We have humus and oxygen,
animals and all the colours.
We have distant lands and bicycles.
We have sun and shadow.
We are rich."

t: Hundertwasser in the jungle in New Zealand, 1994

You can think about what these words mean for you and then write it down or record it.

NATURE: How do you feel when you are surrounded by nature? How important is nature for you? What do you like about nature? Maybe that you can run as fast and as far as you like, that you can climb trees, that you can enjoy a swim in the lake, or that it sometimes rains and snows. And what else?

BEAUTY: What do you find beautiful? There are bound to be pictures, objects or people that you find beautiful. Colours are beautiful, too. But perhaps it is also lovely to have a party, to listen to a story, to dance to wild music, to solve a puzzle in peace and quiet? What do you find beautiful or lovely?

HAPPINESS: What is happiness for you? When are you happy? Can you remember the happiest time in your life?

If you like, you can also think about the opposite. For example:

What do I find really ugly, hideous, really disgusting? What does unhappiness mean to you, when are you not at all happy?

Hundertwasser once said:

> "Beauty is a cure for all ills."

In other words, a sort of medicine which will make everything better again. He didn't really mean it would cure illnesses like coughs and colds, but that it would cure those things which make our souls sick.

745   *BLOBS GROW IN BELOVED GARDENS, 1975*

A pile of poo!

A cycle is something which always comes back to the beginning again.

It carries on running and running, without a beginning and without an end, round and round in a circle. **In nature there are many different sorts of cycle.** When the water from the sea, the rivers and the lakes evaporates in the heat of the sun, it rises into the air. Up in the sky the water then gathers to form a cloud, and from the cloud it rains again back down onto the Earth, back into the seas, the lakes and the rivers, and then the cycle starts all over again.

(692A)   *THE RAIN FALLS FAR FROM US, 1972*

Just think how brilliantly it all works. The plants need the rain in order to live. If the water were to remain in the sea all the time, the plants would die of thirst.

Birth and death form one of the great cycles of nature.

A plant grows and becomes green, it blossoms, bears fruits, becomes barren and dies. But that isn't a cycle, is it? How can the whole thing start again, then?

Apple pips, for example, are the **seeds** of the apple, which will grow into tiny apple trees. But what happens to the rest? When the leaves and the ripe apples fall from the trees and end up lying on the ground, they rot and decompose into tiny little bits and then **become earth once more**. And seeds can fall on this earth again and … you know what happens after that. That is the cycle. But if an apple doesn't fall to the ground, if you eat it up – what happens then? **A pile of poo, of course!** Our body turns it into poo that we flush down the lavatory, and it's gone. Gone? Where does it go? What happens to it?

Look at page 95!

Just as the apples or the leaves can become **humus** so can our poo. Humus is a special sort of earth which is very rich in nutrients. It's fantastic. We form part of the cycle of nature if our poo is allowed to be transformed into humus. **We get our food from nature and in return we give it the nutrients it needs**. But it doesn't work if we flush everything down the lavatory. It may be practical and it doesn't smell, but our poo doesn't get put back in the earth. We interrupt the cycle. And then we are no longer part of nature.

Friedensreich Hundertwasser thought a lot about this problem. He always tried hard to remind people that we are part of a wonderful cycle. You can also imagine a healthy cycle like a rubber hair band. When it breaks it isn't just a bit broken, it's useless.

In order to repair this broken cycle between man and nature, Hundertwasser had an idea. He drew a plan of how to make a **humus lavatory**. It works beautifully and he really used it!

HUNDERT WASSERS WOODEN HUMUS TOILET 1982 1983

ALWAYS OPEN

A LID IS SOMETIMES NEEDED TO KEEP MOISTURE WHEN YOU ARE AWAY OR TO KILL FLIES FOR 10 MINUTES WITH A NOT NOXIOUS SPRAY (PYRETHRUM?) BUT IF WASTE IS WELL COVERED WITH MOIST (NOT WET) HUMUS THER IS NO SMELL AND NO FLIES.

MARINE PLY WOOD

HUMUS SHIT HUMUS SHIT

TOILET SEAT

HUMUS HUMUS ROTTING GARBIDGE HUMUS
SHIT SHIT COVERED WITH HUMUS SHIT
HUMUS ONE BUCKETT FULL OF
SHIT KITCHEN WASTE
STRAW AIRY THIN WOOD CHIPS SMALL
TWIGS LEAF MOULD POROUS HUMUS
← AIR → WOOD
PLASTIC SHEET FOR SAFE DRIPP OFF INTO WATERPROOF TRAY

LOOSE BATTONS LAID ACROSS THE INSIDE FRAME

SLIDE STOP UNDER

HUMUS TOILET – DRAWING FOR THE CONSTRUCTION AND THE USE, 1980

"I built it to show how you can turn your own poo into gold, to make me pleased and to see that it really works – that way, I can sleep more peacefully at night."

Hundertwasser used a humus lavatory in all his houses

Gold? What he meant when he said that was that poo is **something very precious.** It is a part of life. If it can be turned into humus, then new life will be created. And that is a miracle.

The garden dwarf

When some people lay out a garden in the middle of a town or out in the country, they sometimes put dwarfs among the plants. Have you ever seen any? They are little figures and are easy to see because of their pointed caps. They often hold garden tools and smile cheerfully at their surroundings.

Friedensreich Hundertwasser once said:

"Long before history was ever recorded, we were able to talk to the birds, the animals, the plants and the trees, indeed even to water, rocks and clouds, and communication brought harmony. Thus it is written in fairy tales. The garden gnome, together with the elves, pixies, gnomes, giants and the whole host of magical beings, is a last survivor from that distant past. We may now be very "intelligent", but we have forgotten the language of nature. Hence the small gnome in the garden."

The dwarf's purpose, therefore, is to speak with nature on behalf of us humans. But what do humans want to say to nature? Or what questions would they like to ask? Hundertwasser thought about these things too.

"When people feel that they have been unfair to nature, they might put a dwarf in the garden as an apology. He is so small, because grass and flowers are small; he is so small that he can speak better to the snails, animals and plants, as that's something we can't do any more."

Look at page 94!

Many of Hundertwasser´s posters are to do with nature conservation:

775A ARCHE NOAH 2000 – YOU ARE A GUEST OF NATURE – BEHAVE, 1981

808B HAINBURG – FREE NATURE IS OUR FREEDOM, 1984

Why did Friedensreich Hundertwasser believe that humans had wronged nature? I am sure you have heard of **environmental pollution**. It occurs, for example, because we humans produce a great deal of rubbish and it is not easy to get rid of it all. And sometimes it isn't just that it lies around and looks dreadful, but also that it damages nature and poisons it.

Hundertwasser thought:

> "If man wants to have a clean conscience, he must strive for a garbage-free society. He is nature's guest and should behave accordingly. We are all responsible for our garbage. Sorting and making new use of refuse is a beautiful and joyous activity."

 SAVE THE WHALES, 1982

 AMONG TREES YOU ARE AT HOME, 1999

 CHILDREN AND THE ENVIRONMENT, c. 1987

It isn't enough just to get a dwarf to apologise on our behalf – we have to do something! Hundertwasser was an active supporter of nature conservation, not only with his inventions, but also with possibilities he had as an artist. He designed posters.

We have to take care of nature and look after it. Water should be clean, plants should be healthy and animals should be allowed to live a good life. It is up to us humans to see to it. Because nature gives us a great deal. It gives us food and clothing, air to breathe and water to drink. We use wood from trees to build houses and bridges, and we use it to make paper, for example the paper on which this book is printed, or the pencils you use to draw and write. We get all the raw materials which we require from nature.

All day long

Do people who talk like that really get the most out of life? They are in a hurry, want to get things done, rush from one place to the next. They say they have no time. And the more they rush, the shorter and unhappier their day seems to be. It seems as if we can either lose time or take time.

Hundertwasser always took time for his paintings, his thoughts and his dreams. You already know that he sometimes worked on a painting for several years. It seems surprising, then, that he managed to produce so many pictures, posters, prints, drawings, stamps, houses, flags, coins, written works. It seems like magic! After all, we hear all the time that we need to hurry if we want to achieve anything.

But the best things simply take time.

It is easy to understand this if we **take a look at plants**. If a seed falls onto the earth it will begin to germinate. It will grow and **at some point** the tiny leaves will burst through the soil. **Weeks will pass** before it grows into a blossoming flower which delights us with its scent and colours. And if the seed is to grow into an apple tree we shall need to be patient **for years** before we can pick the first apple.

MARCHING GRASS – ON THE MARCH, 1987

Cress is ideal if you want to watch seeds germinate and grow. You can buy the seeds in any supermarket. At home you need some cotton wool; moisten it with water and place it on a saucer. Then put the cress seeds on top. After an hour a jelly-like skin will have formed around each tiny seed. Keep your seeds moist over the next few days and you will be able to watch them sprout and grow. When the cress is about seven centimetres tall you can harvest it and use it in a salad or make yourself a cress sandwich.

Painting pictures is also like a plant growing.

A thought, a feeling, a sentence which somebody said – or something else – arouses in an artist the feeling of wanting to paint a picture. He doesn't know how, but the seed has fallen on the ground and has begun to grow. In order to prepare himself for painting, Hundertwasser would get out paper and paints or would stretch a canvas. Then he would produce a few lines or coloured shapes, as if the first shoots of a plant were beginning to push their way through the earth's surface. And his pictures were as different as plants are. Some blossomed after only a short time and some needed years to find their final form.

Each individual has **his or her own way,** of dealing with time. Some people like to do things slowly to savour every moment of what they are doing. Others prefer to finish something quickly and without fuss and then to take a short break.

Only people who don't take a break, who don't find the time to let an idea germinate, will find it difficult to create something new. They probably want to get from A to B in the shortest possible time. They need straight lines, roads without bends where you can drive as fast as you can.

Hundertwasser in his studio in Spiegelgasse in Vienna, August 1973

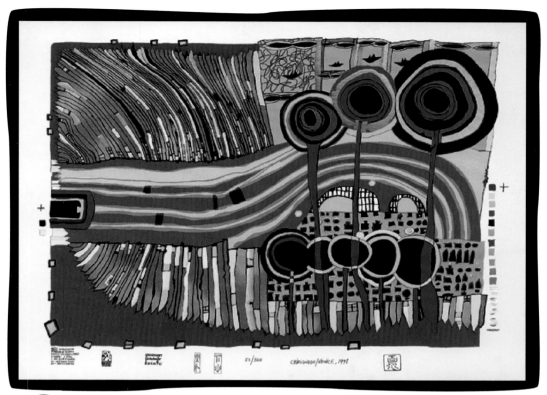

964   *964 FENCES – THE SMALL BARRIER OF BEAUTY, 1998*

Hundertwasser wanted to put up little obstacles to beauty everywhere: either to place such beautiful things along the roadside that people simply had to stop – or obsta-cles which made people slow down in order to **make them aware** of the beautiful things in life. Like an uprooted tree on a foot- path. It makes us stop. There is no need to complain about it – we can also be pleased about it. Perhaps on the detour which we have to take we then discover something which we would otherwise never have seen: a beautiful blossom, a spe- cial fungus on a tree, or a tiny frog. Who knows? The tree is an obstacle which holds us up and shows us something beautiful which we would have missed in our haste to get on. It is an obstacle to beauty.

Look at page 96!

Hundertwasser in front of his ship Regentag, 1989

Travelling is a wonderful experience. You pack your bags and set off. Some people travel by car or by plane; others travel by bike or take the train. You can even go on a short journey on foot.

It is exciting to set off for unknown regions and foreign cities. What will they look like? What sort of people live there? Will I learn something new? **Curiosity** leads you on a voyage of discovery to an unknown country. Friedensreich Hundertwasser travelled a great deal. His first big journey took him to **Italy**, where he met an artist from France who became one of his best friends – René Brô.

Hundertwasser with his artist friend René Brô in front of a mural which they painted together, St. Mandé, 1950

He lived in **France**, or to be more precise, in Paris. Hundertwasser went back with him, because at the time Paris was an important place for many artists, and he ended up living and working there for some time. But then he set off again. He travelled on and on, throughout the whole world. During the course of his life he travelled right round the world … but he often returned to Austria.

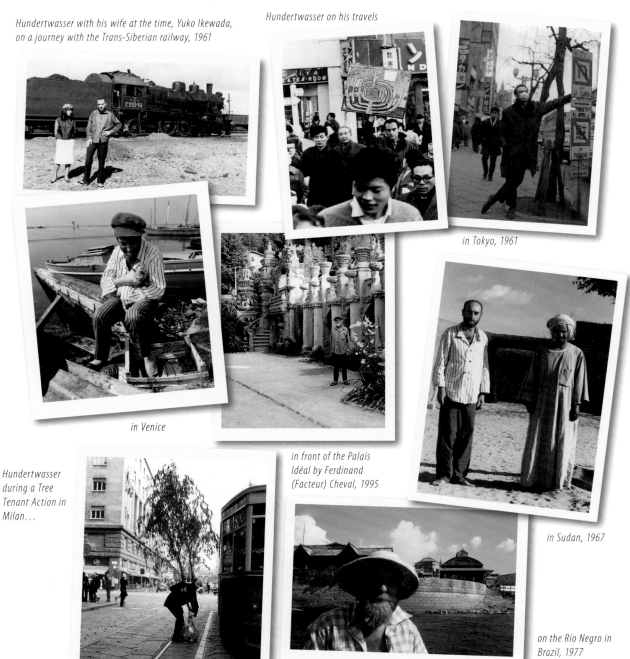

Hundertwasser with his wife at the time, Yuko Ikewada, on a journey with the Trans-Siberian railway, 1961

Hundertwasser on his travels

in Tokyo, 1961

in Venice

in front of the Palais Idéal by Ferdinand (Facteur) Cheval, 1995

Hundertwasser during a Tree Tenant Action in Milan…

in Sudan, 1967

on the Rio Negro in Brazil, 1977

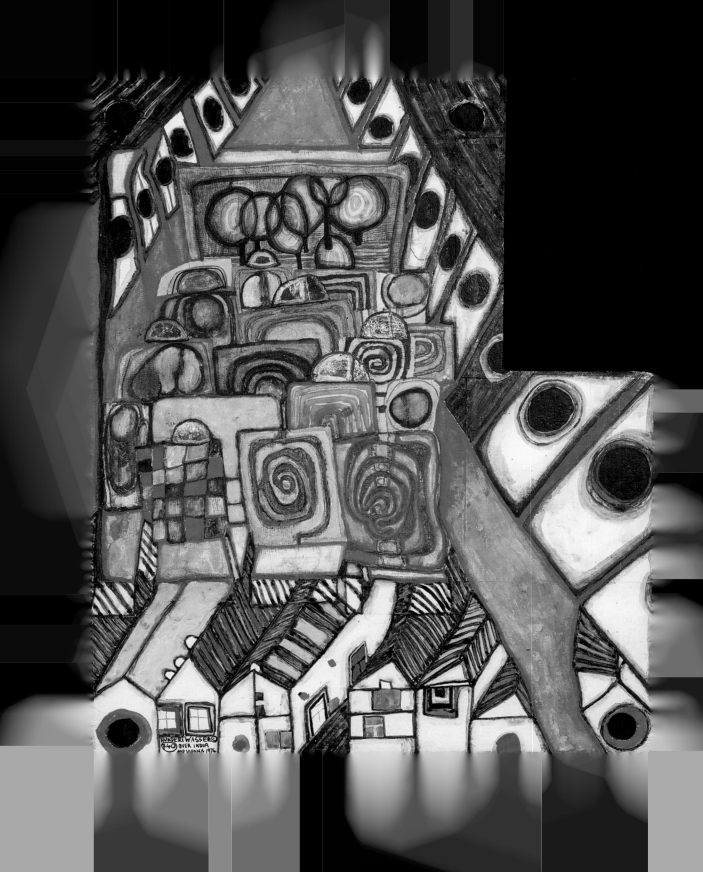

The world is a big place and every little corner of it looks different.

Anyone who sets off on a long journey gets to know foreign cultures and people.

Hundertwasser visited many countries and was richly rewarded with impressions and ideas.

He made many friends and witnessed rare natural spectacles.

While he was travelling he painted and made his experiences visible.

 ON THE RED ROADS OF THE MOUNTAINS OF THE MOON, 1967

In exchange, he spread his message everywhere he went:

The earth can be a paradise and people can be as happy as kings living respectfully

in harmony with nature. In some countries he was invited to make his visions come true.

So he designed buildings and planted trees …

In 1980 Hundertwasser started a tree-planting campaign in Washington.

785A RAINBOW WINDOWS, 1979

847B TREATY WITH NATURE, 1983

557F DO NOT WAIT HOUSES – MOVE, 2000

657A NOCHE DE LA BEBEDORA (THE NIGHT OF THE WOMAN DRINKER), 1967

770A CABO VERDE STEAMER, 1982

… designed stamps – his childhood dream – and invented flags.

862 THE KORU FLAG FOR NEW ZEALAND, 1983

863 PEACE FLAG FOR THE HOLY LAND, 1978

One day he wanted to be alone. He bought a ship, repaired it and changed it to his liking. When it was finished and ready to sail, he gave it a name. He called it REGENTAG.

"On a voyage like this you mostly see the horizon. The horizon is a great point of reference. The horizon is something you can cling to. One really only needs the horizon – everything else can be invented."

Hundertwasser on his boat Regentag

"Sails can have many colours;
red and green, striped and checked.
When I see sails I think of the long voyage."

Do you know what the **horizon** is? It's the furthest line which we can see – exactly the point where **the sky and the earth meet each other**. Especially across **water** you can see a long way. You really get a feeling of **distance and freedom** when you can see over endless distances.

It makes you want to set off at once and go on a journey. When you feel the **spirit of adventure**, you sense a tightness in your chest – it is almost like a slight pain. We sometimes call it "itchy feet", too, or the "call of the wild" – and you can feel the pull all the same.

Look at page 96!

756   *ANTIPODE ISLAND, 1975*

Even if we can't go on a journey, we can still daydream. In the **world of imagination** there are no limits to the journeys we can make. All you need is a horizon. You can invent the sky above it. Perhaps you will imagine a voyage by ship. You set sail on a sunny day, but soon dark storm clouds gather above you and immediately you are caught up in an adventure. And where will your imaginary journey take you? Are you sailing across the South Seas? Or do you manage to scramble onto an iceberg in the Arctic Ocean just in time? But no, suddenly you no longer feel the deck planks beneath your feet. You seem to be sitting on a donkey, your faithful beast of burden, Benny, who has served you loyally on some of your previous journeys. Where is the journey going to take you today?

You could **draw** your own **souvenir photos** of your most exciting foreign trips **yourself**. Take a piece of card the size of a postcard and draw on it. On the other side you can write a message or greetings. Why not put your cards on a pin-board or in an album? Or write your address on the card, stick a stamp on it and post it to yourself. Then you can wait and see whether the secret adventurer or expedition member inside you will write again.

998B   *SPIRAL ON POSTCARD, 1956*

998A   *HEAD ON POSTCARD, 1956*

But Friedensreich Hundertwasser went in search of a **new place to live** on the other side of the world. When he was still a child his mother had told him stories about faraway countries. He remembered years later:

"She talked about New Zealand, that it was a beautiful country where the people are pleasant and where there is no war."

Hundertwasser's "Mountain Hut" on his land in New Zealand, completed in 1995

He searched the world for a **special place** and actually found it in New Zealand. In the language of the original inhabitants, **new Zealand** is called **Ao Tea Roa – The Land of the White Cloud**.

There, beside a gentle stream, Friedensreich Hundertwasser built a house, surrounded by wild, unspoilt nature.

"To land here is to arrive in another world."

Hundertwasser's "Bottlehouse" on his land in New Zealand, built in 1979 with walls made of glass bottles and a grass roof.

He felt at home there. He could paint and think and be what he liked being best, **an artist and plant magician**, who conjured up paintings with magical vegetation.

The pigsty converted by Hundertwasser in 1994/95 on his land in New Zealand; the walls are built of earth tiles and pieces of timber.

Hundertwasser in the New Zealand jungle in about 1974

Farewell

The secrets have been revealed. On your journey through the realm of the painter–king you have acquired a new name and danced outside on a rainy day. You have dug up some treasure and found out about spirals, and hopefully had your interest aroused so that you want to discover still more.

Throughout this entire book, as promised, we have had a look at the art and ideas of Friedensreich Regentag Dunkelbunt Hundertwasser. He hopes that he has encouraged you to develop your interest further and to use your own ideas to change the world. That way it can become a wonderful paradise in which everyone can feel like a king or queen.

Hundertwasser as a child ...

... designing the building blocks for an architecture game.

... painting ...

... on a walk in the Kaurinui Valley in New Zealand, 1999 ...

... as a young man with a child ...

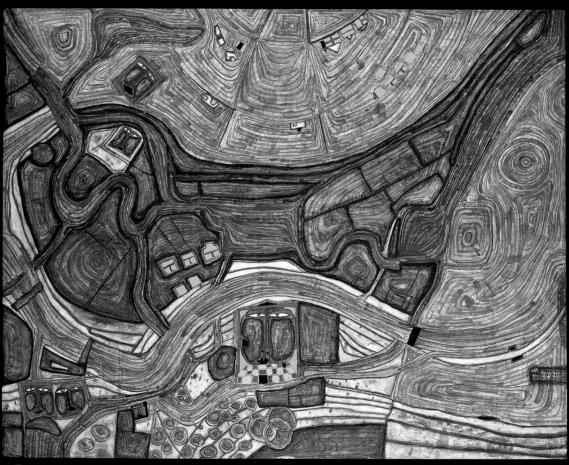

778   *FREDERICK'S FARM, 1978*

Friedensreich Hundertwasser
Painter – Architect – Ecologist – Forerunner
Born in 1928 in Vienna
Died in 2000 on the way from New Zealand to Europe
on board the Queen Elizabeth 2
His life was his message

Photographic credits:
All photographic material was kindly made available by the
Hundertwasser Archives or has been taken from the Publisher's
archives.
Rolf M. Aagaard: 45; Baar: 86 bottom left; Gerhard Deutsch: 49;
Johann Klinger: 12, 15, 72; Herbert Kluger: 58–59; Doris Kutsch-
bach: 9, 18, 19 top, 28, 42 right, 43; Peter Mosdzen: 50, 51, 53, 54;
Sanjiro Minamikawa: 4, 34, 36; Ernst Schauer: 52; Alfred Schmid:
60, 86 top right; Shunk-Kender: 16; Richard Smart: 85 top; Gerhard
Krömer: 20; Vogue: 45; Ludwig Windstosser: 19 bottom, 48;
Konrad Wothe: 42 left; www.zwergshop.ch: 67.
The cover was designed using a photo by Sanjiro Minamikawa
and the work by Hundertwasser 532 *The Lion of Venice*, 1962.

The architects responsible for the project planning of
Hundertwasser's architecture are:
*Residential Building of the City of Vienna, Hundertwasser House,
Austria:* A Hundertwasser Architecture Project, original
coauthor em. o. Univ.-Prof. Arch. DI Josef Krawina,
Planning: DI Peter Pelikan, architect
The Forest Spiral of Darmstadt, Germany: Heinz M. Springmann,
architect
In the Meadows Bad Soden, Germany: Peter Pelikan, architect
District Heating Plant Spittelau, Vienna/Austria: Waagner Biró –
Marchart, Moebius & Partner, Vienna; Planning of the façade:
Peter Pelikan, architect
The Green Citadel of Magdeburg, Germany: Peter Pelikan, architect;
execution on site: Heinz M. Springmann, architect

Prestel is a member of Verlagsgruppe Random House GmbH
Prestel Verlag, Munich
www.prestel.de

Prestel Publishing Ltd.
14–17 Wells Street
London W1T 3PD
Tel. +44 (0)20 7323-5004
Fax +44 (0)20 7323-0271

Prestel Publishing
900 Broadway, Suite 603
New York, N.Y. 10003
Tel. +1 (212) 995-2720
Fax +1 (212) 995-2733

www.prestel.com

Prestel books are available worldwide. Please contact your
nearest bookseller or one of the above addresses for information
concerning your local distributor.

The Library of Congress Cataloguing-in-Publication data is
available.
British Library Cataloguing-in-Publication Data: a catalogue
record for this book is available from the British Library.
The Deutsche Bibliothek holds a record of this publication
in the Deutsche Nationalbibliografie; detailed bibliographical
data can be found under: http://dnb.d-nb.de

Editorial direction by Doris Kutschbach
Translated by Jane Michael, Munich
Copy-edited by Christopher Wynne, Bad Tölz
Design and layout by Michael Schmölzl,
agenten.und.freunde, Munich
Typeset by Wolfram Söll, Munich
Origination by Repro Ludwig, Zell am See
Printed and bound by Neografia, Bratislava

Verlagsgruppe Random House FSC®N001967.
The FSC®-certified paper *Hello Fat Matt 1,1* has been
supplied by Condat, Le Lardin Saint-Lazare, France

ISBN 978-3-7913-4098-2

Things to make and do

Get your inspiration here!
Would you like to see exactly how things decompose,
build a house of boxes, or make and do things with paints, paintbrushes, crayons, scissors
and other materials?

Here you will find plenty of suggestions as to how you can use Hundertwasser's ideas and
works of art to be creative yourself.

Your treasure chest

* read about it on page 9

Have you also got a stamp collection? Or do you collect pretty stones,
shells, bouncy balls, erasers?
Would you like to make a really nice treasure chest to keep your treasures in?

You could use a cardboard box or a little wooden chest. Depending on how secret you want to make it, you
can decorate either only the inside or both the inside and outside. As material
you could use wrapping paper, fabric, trimmings, buttons, shiny aluminium foil, photos or pictures from
magazines which you can stick on.

You can keep everything you find beautiful in your treasure
chest. When you are feeling sad or on days when everything
seems to be going wrong, get your treasure chest out and look
at your precious things. They will make you feel a bit better.

Feeling colours

* read about it on page 28

One colour is not the same as another! Depending on the materials you use, your pictures will end up looking quite different from each other.

This is how you can see and feel the difference between chalk, pencil, paints, paintbrushes, paper and every thing else you can think of:
Paint the same picture – a car, a tree, your family, whatever you feel like painting – several times using different materials.
How does it feel when you paint with a brush or draw with a felt-tipped pen, or with a pencil or a ballpoint pen? Which background do you think goes best with which material?
Do you need more space on your paper if you use finger paints or if you use chalk?
How does it change what you paint?

Rubbing

* read about it on page 43

Rubbing is a fantastic technique which you can use to make the surface and structure of an object visible. If you think a surface looks interesting, all you need to do is to lay a sheet of paper on top and then shade gently over the entire surface with a pencil or a crayon. As if by magic, a pattern will appear on the paper. You can achieve interesting results with coins, leaves, wooden floors and different woven fabrics.
Why not go looking for different patterns! Your sense of touch will help you find them.

Bright, bright, bright

* read about it on page 39

Hundertwasser's favourite colours were "dark-bright". Which colours do you like best?

Colours look quite different, depending on how we put them together.
Try, for example, what bright red looks like next to various other colours:
it shines especially brightly next to green.
And what about yellow?

Which colour contrasts do you like best?
Do you like seeing several similar colours together? Try it out – perhaps by painting a picture
of water using various shades of blue.
Or do you like multi-coloured pictures – greens, reds, blues and yellows all mixed up together?
Do you prefer soft, light colours?
Or do you go for bold shades?

Here are two tips for especially brilliant pictures

Paint a picture in your favourite colours with oil pastels or wax crayons.
When you have finished, paint over the whole thing with black or dark blue watercolour.
In the places where you have used greasy pastels or crayons the watercolour will not
adhere to the paper – and the brightly coloured lines will shine brightly against the
dark background!

Sugared chalk also produces brilliant colours: for this you simply have to soak whole
sticks of coloured chalk in sugar water until they have absorbed as much liquid as
possible and feel really damp. Paint on dark coloured paper.
At the beginning it won't look very special, but as soon as the chalks dry on the paper
the colours will begin to glow!

Your second skin Design your own T-shirt!

* read about it on page 45

Do you want something absolutely unique to wear?
Talk to your parents: there are a few good ways of transforming a plain T-shirt into a
distinctive, very personal item of clothing.

You can paint directly onto fabric using textile colours. The picture will
remain visible even after you wash the T-shirt.
Put a sheet of card or plastic between the layers of fabric before you start,
so that the colour doesn't run through.

You can also buy some special paper which you can draw or paint on using normal pencils and wax crayons.
Then the picture can be ironed onto the fabric.
It appears as a mirror-image on the T-shirt – so be careful if you want to write a message!

You can also make a collage of pictures you have drawn, photos and other pictures. Cut them out as you like
and stick them onto a sheet of paper. Using it as a pattern you can go to a copy shop and they will copy it onto a T-shirt.
It's a very quick method, but it isn't exactly cheap.

Mosaics

* read about it on page 59

Have you ever seen a mosaic? A mosaic is made up of lots of tiny pieces.
Usually these are of stone, glass or ceramic. For centuries mosaics have been
used to decorate floors, walls and other objects.

In order to try it out at home, it is much easier to make small snippings of coloured paper or
cut photos from magazines into small pieces. Sort them according to colour. Then you need a sheet
of paper and some paste. Now arrange the little pieces of paper to make a pretty picture or pattern. It's rather
like a jigsaw puzzle. When you are satisfied with your picture you can stick the pieces of mosaic onto the paper.

A house just for you

* read about it on page 56

What would it look like? Tall and narrow or low and wide? Round or angular?
With turrets and decorative frills?

Invent a house and make a model of it!
The best building materials are things you have found or which have been
thrown away: cheese boxes, detergent bottles, toothpicks, milk cartons,
coffee tins, yoghurt tubs, polystyrene . . .
You will find lots of things which will be ideal for making your dream house.

You can cover the outside with paper and paint it or decorate it in some way.
If you like doing this, why not design an entire town?

The shoe-box house

* read about it on page 58

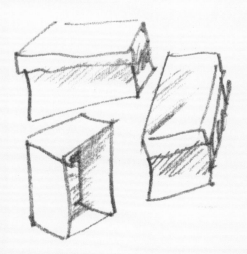

Would you like to build a box house?
Shoe boxes are the best building material. If you cut a hole in the bottom
of the shoe box and pile several on top of each other, you can make a sort of
block of flats.

You can decorate the windows and the walls of the individual rooms with different
materials. You can paint them or stick fabric on them, cover them with silver foil or
sew on buttons, whatever you like. Who do you think would like to live in this house?

Your very own window

* read about it on page 53

What would a window look like if you were to design it exactly as you like? You can try out your ideas here!

Elves, dwarfs and friends

*read about it on page 67

Next time you go for a walk or a hike in the country or in the park you can collect material to invent your own little character which is close to nature. It doesn't have to be a garden dwarf – it could be a mountain troll or a water nymph or a creature which you have thought up yourself.

You can use twigs and leaves, bark, moss and stones, grass stalks, conkers and pine cones to make a figure. Cotton thread or string and glue will probably be useful to hold everything together.

Or you could draw your little friend. At the same time you could also paint where it lives and what its friends look like.

Composting experiments

* read about it on page 65

Maybe you would like to watch things rot or decompose more closely?

You need an empty glass jar and some earth. Put
a layer of earth about 2–3 cm thick in the jar. Then
add a chopped-up salad leaf and a slice of apple or
some kitchen refuse like potato peelings on top.
Add a few drops of water but not too much – it
shouldn't swim in water. Then screw on the lid.
That isn't necessary for the contents to rot, but it
will make sure that it doesn't smell and attract
flies – they love the smell of rotting vegetables.
Open the lid from time to time and allow some air
to enter the jar.

Now you can watch what happens. It is an experiment which needs
patience on your part. You won't notice anything immediately the next
day. You could make a diary of the decomposition and write down what
you can see like a scientist.

When the decomposition is complete or you don't want to continue
with the experiment, don't just throw the jar in the bin, but return the
result to nature. That is what Hundertwasser wanted to remind us: that
we are all part of nature.

"Little obstacles to beauty"

*read about it on page 73

You can make a "beauty barrier" too!
All you need is a few sticks of pavement chalk. Draw a pretty picture on the pavement in front of your house. And there you have your beauty barrier!

Watch how the passers-by react to your picture. Who stops to look at it? Who walks round it? And who doesn't seem to notice your picture and just walks over it?

The ship of wishes

*read about it on page 81

In order to keep your itchy feet on the ground you can make a "ship of wishes" from paper. How? Paint, draw and write your wishes on a sheet of paper. You can use both the front and the back of the sheet. Then fold the paper to make a paper boat as in the diagrams below. When you pass some flowing water you can let your boat sail away. And your wishes will set off on their journey.

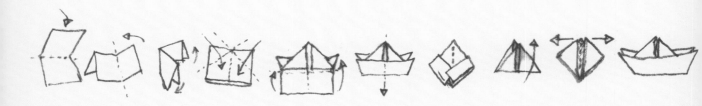

Your boat, your sail

* read about it on page 81

If you had a boat which you could sail across the seas in, what would the sails look like? Would they be patterned in bright colours or plain black like the sails of a pirate ship? Or would you have pink sails with flowers on them? Draw the sailing boat of your dreams and give it a name.